Beginner's Guide to
Machine Embroidered
Flowers

Dedication
To Tom and Jon, with love

Beginner's Guide to
Machine Embroidered
Flowers

Alison Holt

First published in Great Britain 2006

Search Press Limited
Wellwood, North Farm Road,
Tunbridge Wells, Kent TN2 3DR

Text copyright © Alison Holt 2006

Photographs by Steve Crispe, Search Press Studios
and Myk Briggs, myk@thebakery
Photographs and design copyright © Search Press Ltd. 2006

ISBN: 1 84448 058 5

Suppliers
If you have difficulty in obtaining any of the materials and equipment mentioned in this book, please visit our website at www.searchpress.com.

Publisher's note
All the step-by-step photographs in this book feature the author, Alison Holt, demonstrating machine embroidery. No models have been used.

All the embroideries are reproduced approximately actual size unless stated otherwise.

Manufactured by Universal Graphics Pte Ltd, Singapore
Printed in Malaysia by Times Offset (M) Sdn Bhd

I would like to thank my students for their enthusiasm and for asking so many questions, making me think about my embroideries and my teaching and therefore helping me to produce books that hopefully supply a lot of the answers.

Also, thank you to Katie Chester, my editor, for her tremendous input and support. It was a real pleasure to work with her on this book.

Finally, a big thank you to Myk Briggs for being so generous with his time and knowledge.

Front cover
Eryngiums and Daisies
See pages 48–49.

Page 1
Delphiniums and Roses
A wide range of techniques was used for this small, detailed embroidery.

Page 2
Rudbekia
A good example of 'drawing' with a varying width of zigzag stitch on the petals and leaves.

Page 3
Through the Rose Arch
The brick pillar and path are painted silk (smooth detail) and everything else is stitched (textured detail).

Contents

Datura Lilies

A painted background of leaves and two other lilies give depth to this image. This is a good example of 'painting' with stitches in a subtle way, with parallel rows of straight stitch following the shape of the flower.

Introduction

This is a guide to drawing flowers and their foliage with a sewing machine, using colour, line and texture on a delicate scale. It has wonderful possibilities and potential for the beginner as well as for the more experienced embroiderer.

Using the machine as a versatile drawing tool, with straight stitch used as a fine line and zigzag stitch as a broad line which can vary in width along its length, is the strength and appeal of machine embroidery for me. It can be used to produce a fine and delicate line of strong colour that, on this scale, would be impossible with a brushstroke of paint. Textured, raised stitches standing proud of the fabric add richness and depth to a picture, and can enhance the sense of perspective. Used in conjunction with silk-painted backgrounds, embroidery is an exciting medium to work in.

I am a keen gardener; it's a wonderful contrast to sitting indoors at a sewing machine for many hours at a time. A lot of the photographs and embroideries in this book are based on the three-dimensional creation outside my house: my garden. It is a constant source of inspiration for me. I grow foxgloves, delphiniums, rhododendrons, irises, alliums, roses and much more, and try to create groupings of plants and views with embroideries in mind. As I weed or deadhead, I look at all the different flowers and imagine the techniques I could use on the machine to recreate them in

Astilbe and Dogwood

Detail taken from original measuring 18 x 13cm (7 x 5in)
The complementary colours red and green work well in this richly textured study of flowers and foliage.

stitch. My visits to the Chelsea and Hampton Court flower shows as an exhibitor give me wonderful opportunities to collect ideas for my garden as well as my embroideries.

People look at my embroideries and make a range of comments, and the most common misconception is that I use a computerised embroidery machine that somehow creates a 'shortcut' between my photographs and sketches and the finished piece. Some people assume I use the embroidery stitches available on all machines, and simply repeat the same size and shape of flower or leaf over and over again. But nature isn't as predictable as this – which is why all my work is produced by drawing freely with a sewing machine.

For me, the difference between freehand embroidery and computer-aided design for embroidery is the choice between using your skills as an artist to draw with the sewing machine, or learning how to use software on a computer to produce the effect you want. Computer-generated embroidery has its place, and it can be combined with other techniques to great effect. But as clever and as effective as it is, I prefer to be a creative machine embroiderer.

My aim is to create embroidered flowers, each one unique. It is achieved by analysing the shapes and colours of the flowers and breaking down the embroidery into simple steps. I decide whether straight stitch or zigzag will provide the technique I need, or perhaps a combination of the two. I also consider the direction, length and colour of stitch that I will use. With the help of this book, I hope that you too will find the inspiration and technical know-how you need to create your own embroidered flowers.

Chelsea Garden

An award-winning garden at Chelsea was the inspiration for this embroidery. The composition is divided into horizontal sections, the central one being a painted area of closely clipped lawn which serves to break up the two areas of embroidery and to give a smooth background for the foreground detail. The diversity of plants in the border required a broad range of embroidery techniques.

Materials and equipment

Advice on the equipment needed for creative machine embroidery can be invaluable, for example the best sewing machine to use, the right size and type of hoop, which threads, and so on. Information about materials, which may not be essential but make life easier or provide a shortcut, can also be a great help. This section aims to pass all this information on to you, to enable you to move on to the next stage of producing some embroidery.

Sewing machine

Creative embroidery can be done using any electric sewing machine. You can create more textures if your machine has a swing needle which does zigzag as well as straight stitch. A dial for controlling stitch width is better than push buttons as it allows you to alter the stitch width smoothly and therefore to 'draw' with a line of varying width.

Some sewing machines are set into a table, which is ideal. If this is not an option then a table attachment is important. It supports the hoop as you work, allowing you to slide the hoop around on the table. This is especially helpful when guiding the hoop with one hand as you alter the stitch width control with the other.

You can adapt your machine for embroidery by making only a few simple changes. First remove the presser foot. This will allow you to move the embroidery in any direction. Then lower the feed dog, which usually feeds the fabric through the machine in a straight line and is linked with the stitch length control. You will then be able to move your embroidery freely in different directions and at different speeds. This will enable you to create different lengths of stitch simply by varying how fast you move your embroidery; move it slowly to make small stitches and quickly for larger stitches.

Bobbin case

Some people are nervous about altering the tension screw on a bobbin case, and purchase a spare one to use for machine embroidery. The case should ideally be removable to allow easy access to the tension screw. Turn the tension screw clockwise to tighten the tension – this will keep the bobbin thread under the embroidery out of sight. Turning it anticlockwise will loosen the tension, enabling the thread in the bobbin to come to the surface of your embroidery and make it visible.

Machine maintenance

Some of the problems people encounter when starting machine embroidery are not due to inexperience but are caused by problems with the machine, which can be avoided if some basic steps are taken.

- A sewing machine needs to be well maintained – a machine that is serviced regularly will give you trouble-free sewing.
- Check your machine is sewing properly before you remove the foot and lower the feed dog.
- Always ensure the needle is sharp. A blunt or bent needle will create problems.
- Clean your machine regularly – lint will build up around the throat plate and needs to be removed.
- Check that the machine is threaded up correctly and that the bobbin is correctly inserted.
- Follow the manufacturer's guide for oiling your machine and do it regularly.

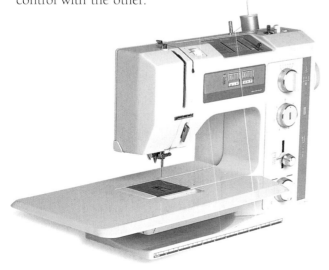

Threads

You can use any type of machine thread for creative embroidery, but there are threads available that are made especially for machine embroidery. These have a beautiful sheen and are available in numerous shades and tones. You will need a good variety of threads; not only a wide range of colours, but also various tones of the same colour. If you've done machine embroidery before, you may well have already started a collection. I use fine, 50 or 40, pure cotton threads in soft, natural colours, but to broaden my colour range I also use good-quality polycotton mixes.

Just some of the coloured threads I use in my embroideries.

Other sewing equipment

Embroidery hoop

To keep fabric flat and prevent puckering or distortion, it should be stretched very tightly in a hoop. If there is any give in it at all, the machine may miss stitches and the thread will fray and eventually break. I use a 20cm (8in) wooden embroidery hoop with a slotted screw which can be tightened with a screwdriver. This maintains a really good tension.

Binding the inner hoop with cotton tape will help grip the silk more effectively, and to some extent prevent the hoop from marking the silk. If the image is larger than the hoop, the embroidery will need to be worked in two or more sections. This means restretching the silk in a different position after completing one section of the embroidery. To further safeguard the silk from marking, make sure you don't position the hoop across a painted area of the image, for example a sky. Plan the positioning of the hoop to avoid areas where marks will show, but if this is not possible, only pull the silk through the hoop where embroidery stitches will eventually sit so that any marks will be covered.

Needles

There are many choices of needle available today – ballpoint, metallic, machine embroidery, etc. I have been using the same needles for 15 years. They are a standard size 80 (12) general-purpose needle and are suitable for the weight of silk I use. The most important quality of any needle is that it is in good condition; a blunt needle will cause pull lines in the silk.

Screwdrivers

Use a small screwdriver to alter the tension on the bobbin case and a larger one to tighten the screw on the hoop.

Embroidery scissors

These need to have sharp, pointed ends so you can cut threads close to the work on the right side of your embroidery. They should also be comfortable to use.

Bobbins

Keep a number of bobbins, each wound with a different colour, ready for use.

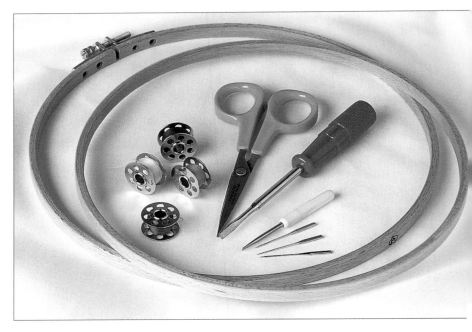

Equipment for transferring the design

Use L-shaped card to crop your photograph when choosing the final size and composition of your design.

Source photograph

This is the starting point – the inspiration – for your design. You may have more than one photograph, and combine various elements of each one in your final composition.

L-shaped card

Use this to try cropping your photograph in different ways before deciding on the final size and composition of your design.

Paper and pencil

You need these to sketch out your initial composition and design ideas, including notes on colour, detail and technique.

Ruler

Use a ruler to make sure the edges of your picture are straight and square. If you are using a ruler to draw a line with resist, be careful not to smudge the wet line when moving the ruler away.

Water/air-soluble pen

This is used to mark out the composition, or the details within it, on the silk. It is air soluble but can be removed more quickly with water. A damp cotton bud works well.

Resist

Resist is a clear gel which, when applied to silk, dries to form a barrier between different areas of dye. It is used to control the flow of the dyes on the silk or mark the positions of elements in the picture. A small pipette with a No. 6 (or 0.3mm) nib attached to the nozzle is ideal, as it produces a very fine line that is still wide enough to contain the dyes. When the painting stage is complete, the resist can be washed out with hot, soapy water.

Marker pen and tracing paper/acetate

Use permanent marker pen to mark out your design on tracing paper or acetate before transferring it to the silk. The thick, black outline will show strongly through the fabric, making it easier to trace over.

Masking tape

You may decide to transfer the design straight from your source photograph. Use masking tape to secure the photograph underneath the silk. When cropping your source photographs to attach pieces of L-shaped card to each other, and to your photograph.

Light box

This is a useful aid for transferring a design on to your silk. Place the tracing or source photograph on the light box with the silk over the top.

Silk painting equipment

Fabric

There is a huge range of silk fabric available. I use 8mm habutai silk, which is of medium weight and has a fine weave and smooth appearance. It is ideal for the painted areas of my embroideries and works very well with the scale of the stitches. If you wish to experiment before starting a design, a lightweight cotton is a good substitute, but remember that dye will behave differently on silk. Also, the thickness of the fabric used has an effect on the look of the stitches at the embroidery stage.

Brushes

I have a range of watercolour brushes from 000 to an 8, the smallest for painting fine details and the largest for flat washes of colour. It is important to use the right size brush for the areas or scale you are painting.

Silk paints/dyes

I prefer the liquid paints or dyes because they change only the colour not the appearance of the silk. Water-based dyes are suitable for silk, cotton and synthetic fabrics. They are available in a wide range of colours, which can be used directly from the bottle. Mix them together to make new colours or add water to make them paler. They can be fixed easily with a hot iron.

Wooden frame

When applying dyes, the silk should first be stretched on a frame. You can use an embroidery hoop, but this will restrict the size of your design. I use a 40cm (16in) square frame, which allows me to paint one large image, or several smaller images.

Silk pins

Silk pins have three small prongs and grip the fabric better than ordinary drawing pins. They are also less likely to tear the fabric.

Palette

I always use a white ceramic palette. Plastic is quickly discoloured by the dyes, and white allows you to see the colours you are mixing.

Hairdryer

Use a hairdryer to dry the outliner so you can move more quickly to the painting stage. It can also be used to dry the dye quickly and prevent it spreading too far.

Iron

Iron the silk for two minutes to fix the dye to the fabric once it is dry.

All the equipment you need for painting a background on to your silk.

Up to the Garden

The softly painted details within the composition
allow the texture of flowers and foliage to stand out.

Design

The first important step to producing a picture is choosing an image and creating a design based on it. Ideas can come from all around you – photographs, sketches and 'found' material. We are all attracted to different images, perhaps because of the colours or texture, detail or some abstract quality; we all have different tastes. It is a good idea initially to be guided by a tutor and to follow design rules, but to then go one step further and make something that is uniquely yours.

Composition

The composition of a picture is the way the various elements within it – shape, colour, texture, and so on – are arranged. When composing your picture, try to create a sense of harmony, with all the different elements working together. Think about the shape of your design: for example, it could be a square, circle, rectangle or oval. To achieve a successful design, you should consider the following four principles.

Contrast

This can be achieved, for example, by combining different textures such as rough and smooth, shiny and matt, or hard and soft. For tonal contrasts use light and dark, or complementary colours such as red and green, purple and yellow, or orange and blue. Also consider the use of contrasting shapes within your design.

Rhythm

Rhythm gives a natural sense of order to a composition. It can be created by repetition, such as waves of bluebells in a wood or poppies in a meadow, or by repeating the same shape or colour along the length of a flower border.

Negative shapes

These are the shapes created between the various elements in the composition. They are a significant part of the design, and should therefore be given the same amount of consideration as the other design components.

Foxgloves and Delphiniums

The shapes and colours of the flowers are repeated along the curve of the flower border, drawing the eye along its length. Contrast is created by embroidering the flower border and painting the lawn.

Balance

The principle of the Golden Section relates to the idea of balance in an asymmetrical composition, and many of my designs acknowledge it.

It is based on our natural tendency to divide a rectangle or a line in the ratio of approximately one-third/two-thirds. This principle can be applied to a picture to determine where to place the focal point; what proportions of the various colours to use; or where to position the horizon. It creates a natural balance with which people will generally feel comfortable.

It is important to take into account balance and proportion when you are beginning to design, but remember that if you are happy with the way your design looks – even if it does not follow any recognised guidelines – you should go with your instincts rather than hard-and-fast rules.

Garden Door

The edge of the door creates contrast and a strong, vertical line, which divides the composition in the ratio one to two. Strong diagonals formed by the foliage lead the eye towards the back of the picture.

Using photographs

I take my camera with me wherever I go. The seasons change and there is always something new to see. From snowdrops and daffodils in the early part of the year, through the colourful summer flowers, to autumn hues and seed heads and berries in the winter. Inspiration is everywhere, all year round.

Sketching or painting is an enjoyable way of recording your ideas. A good shortcut to this is taking photographs. Photographs are a great starting point for your design, providing a composition, detail and colour reference. They can be used in their original state, cropped to improve the balance of the composition, reduced or enlarged in scale. Sometimes the background may not be as colourful as you would like, or certain elements may not be placed naturally for achieving the best balance within the picture – this is an opportunity to be creative!

Daffodils

Small amendments have been made to the background of trees. This has been painted so that the background recedes, giving the picture more depth. The foreground has been cropped to emphasise the density of the daffodils, and the silver birch tree trunks on the left have been bought further into the picture to improve the composition.

Several photographs can be combined to create a new composition. This can be done by joining two or more photographs to create a long, narrow image, or by selecting elements from each photograph and putting them together in a new composition. Because photographic images are a standard size, it is interesting to play around with the dimensions by cropping the sides. For example, a broad, panoramic view could be created by cropping the top and bottom of the picture, or a long, elegant, single flower could be given a tall, narrow frame.

Roadside Poppies

I liked the foreground poppies in the bottom photograph, but the embroidery needed more sky to balance the composition. I therefore combined it with the top right-hand part of the photograph above.

17

Rosebay Willowherb

This composition was taken directly from the top photograph. I took the other photograph to provide a detailed reference for the flowers in the foreground. Studying close-up the structure of the flowers in your composition helps you to decide which embroidery techniques to use.

The Coast Road

This composition was achieved by cropping the photograph as shown by the white lines, and I also enlarged the cow parsley to make the foreground more interesting and to increase the sense of perspective.

Hollyhocks and Pots

A rich mixture of stitched and painted detail was used to make this embroidery. It was based on a village in France full of flowers, narrow steps and beautiful, half-timbered houses. The decision to paint the stonework, steps and pots and to embroider all the flowers and foliage seemed a natural one.

19

Colour

An important step on the way to creating an embroidered picture is learning how to choose colours of threads, and how to mix colours in paint for the background of the design.

Understanding the use of colour

Whether you are working from life or photographs, you need to be able to identify and interpret colours, matching threads and paints so that the embroidery looks as realistic as possible. It therefore helps if you have an understanding of colour and how different colours are linked and composed.

Our perception of colour is altered by perspective, appearing softer, more subdued in the distance, brighter, more intense in the foreground. In the picture opposite, I have made the distant building and foliage much softer and paler in tone, and used stronger, more contrasting colours in the foreground, mirroring the effect of perspective.

Think about how to use colour to dramatic effect. Complementary colours work well together, such as red and green, blue and orange, purple and yellow. The book cover is a good example of this. It is fun to experiment with colours and make them work for you in a composition. Think also about the relative proportions of different colours – the splashes of red amongst the green foliage created by the foreground geraniums in the picture opposite are far more dramatic than a lot of red flowers spread throughout the picture would be.

In the Shade

20

How to choose colours in thread

The appearance of a colour is influenced by the colour next to it. When choosing a range of threads for a picture, I begin by identifying the colours I need within each part of my source photograph. This is best done in natural light, before you start stitching.

I start by holding a reel of thread over the photograph and deciding whether or not it is a good match. Gradually I move from one area of the picture to another, grouping together the threads I need. I then check that the reels of colour I have chosen work well together, and that they echo the range of colour in the photograph; if they don't, I reconsider my choices. I also make sure that the tones are equally spaced between the darkest and the lightest coloured threads. Be bold in your tonal range; the embroidery will not look three-dimensional or strong enough if the dark shades are not really dark and the highlights are not pale enough.

Day Lilies

This picture illustrates how colour, contrast and rhythm work in a composition. The use of complementary colours – red and green, and the softer purples and yellows – gives the picture its sense of drama. With its bold, horizontal bands of colour and the reds, oranges and yellows in the foreground repeated in the distant border, a strong sense of rhythm is created, and the eye is led towards the background.

How to mix colours in paint

A basic understanding of how to mix paint colours is important. In theory, all colours can be mixed from the three primary colours: yellow, blue and red, as show in the colour wheel opposite. Any two primaries mixed together will give a secondary colour: mixed in equal amounts, blue and yellow make green, blue and red make purple and yellow and red make orange. If you vary the proportion of each primary colour, the end result will change. For example, more yellow than blue mixed together will make a lime/yellow-green, and more red than yellow will produce a red-orange.

It is helpful to experiment with mixing colours, and to note down the colours and their proportions, and the end results. This will give you a better understanding of how colour works.

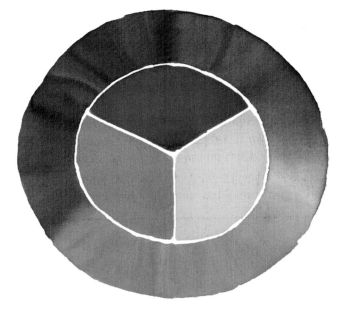

When a primary colour is mixed with a secondary colour, the range of colours increases, and purple-browns, blue-greys and reddish-browns are created. These are called tertiary colours. A small sample of different browns is shown below, created by mixing different proportions of red and green. Adding more yellow or red will change the shade of brown.

Paint a small brushful of paint on to some silk and let it dry. Do this with every colour you have so that you can see the full range. Then mix the secondary colours and move on to other combinations to see what your paints can give you in terms of a colour range. All the colours you produce can then have water added to make them paler, further increasing the range.

Pots of Colour

In this embroidery, tertiary colours have been used effectively to paint the pots and stonework, which serve to emphasise the bright colours of the embroidered flowers.

22

How to blend colours in embroidery

Unlike painting with silk paints, where any shade you want can be mixed, with threads you are limited by the available range. I use several different manufacturers' threads for the simple reason that it extends the range of colours I have to choose from. Even with an extensive range, however, I sometimes can't find the perfect match. If the colour you want lies between two shades, the solution is to put one in the top of the machine and one in the bobbin. With small stitches and the bobbin colour showing on the surface, the two colours are mixed by the eye to the shade you want.

This technique (loose bobbin tension and tight top tension so that the bobbin colour is visible) is also ideal for blending and shading, and has been used to create the subtle changes in colour and tone in the picture opposite. Notice that the more distant flowers are painted. They are 'suggestions' of the intricately embroidered foreground flowers, echoing their shapes and colours for continuity.

The petals above were worked in sections along their length, with the bobbin colour – mid pink – remaining the same and the top thread changing from deep to pale pink. If the bobbin colour is visible, it helps to blend the top colours together. The green leaf was stitched following the same technique – its colour changes from dark green at its base to light green at its tip.

The two petals on the left use the same shading and blending effects, but worked across the petal rather than along its length.

Knapweed (Centaurea nigra)

Parallel rows of straight stitch follow the curve of each slim petal. The order of work was important, completing the petals underneath before the ones on top. Observe the subtle differences in colour of each petal, and also how the colour changes within each petal.

Distance and detail

In some of my embroideries I need to create an illusion or an impression, for example not every flower in a well-stocked border can be embroidered individually. A border of delphiniums, for example, would have a well-observed and executed flower or three in the foreground and lots of tall, textured shapes in blues and purples in the distance. This works equally well for poppies in a field or drifts of snowdrops in a woodland scene.

Foliage is as important and as individual as the flowers themselves. Look at and identify the incredible range of greens, from the deepest blue-greens in the shadows to the palest yellow-green highlight, and everything in-between. A distant area of foliage is created by capturing the essence of it: does it have dissected or broad leaves, is its habit tall and spiky, dense or wispy? How widely do the colours vary? All of these characteristics need to be observed and will require a different technique.

In both the bluebells embroidery below and the snowdrops opposite, foreground detail shows each flower well constructed using closely worked zigzags. As the flowers recede into the distance, they become horizontal bands of colour, giving just the impression of flowers.

I am often asked what technique is used for a particular flower, a foxglove for example. There isn't one answer; so much depends on where it sits in the picture, and therefore how much detail you can see. A foreground foxglove, where you can see the individual trumpet-shaped flowers and many shades of pink, would require a totally different approach to a distant flower that is identified by its overall colour, shape and habit. The skill is in observation, for example foxgloves, in the distance, are tall, slender, tapering shapes that curve over at their tip.

Woodland Walk

Detail taken from original measuring 28 x 10cm (11 x 4in)
The middle distance foxgloves in the embroidery above are more simple in their construction than the foreground ones opposite. They are created with parallel columns of closely worked zigzag hanging down from the central stem of the flower. Working up one side of the foxglove stem and then the other, notice that the columns (trumpets) become shorter towards the top of the flower.

Foxgloves

This close-up study of foxgloves uses a combination of techniques. The trumpets are closely worked zigzags that gradually decrease in width towards the stem. These and the small buds are worked before the stem, which covers the connecting threads. With a darker shade in the bobbin and a tight top tension used so the bobbin thread is visible, the trumpets are shaded at the edges, adding to their three-dimensional quality. Where the zigzag is not wide enough, two overlapping rows are used.

Getting started

A few small adjustments to your sewing machine will be needed before you can use it for creative embroidery.

Removing the presser foot

Removing the presser foot gives you an unobstructed view of your embroidery. Its normal function is to keep the fabric flat on the bed of the machine, but in machine embroidery the fabric is held flat by the hoop in which it is stretched. Remove the presser foot by unclipping or unscrewing it from the base of the presser bar. Some manufacturers recommend using a darning or embroidery foot on the machine, but this is not really necessary.

Lowering the feed dog

This allows you to move your embroidery in any direction and at any speed. Usually there is a dial or switch for lowering the feed dog, which on some machines is the same setting as for darning. If you cannot lower the feed dog, your machine may have a raised plate that fits over the moving teeth. If neither of these is possible, set the stitch length to zero. Each of these options will achieve the same result.

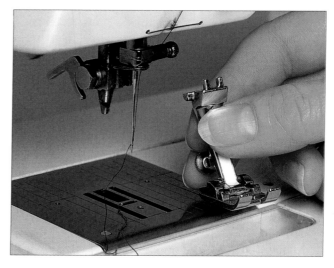

Removing the presser foot. Notice that the feed dog has been lowered so that it is no longer visible.

Tension of the threads

In conventional machine stitching, the tensions of the top and bobbin threads need to be balanced to form the perfect stitch. With machine embroidery, you can create a range of textures and effects by simply altering the tensions.

To change the tension of the bobbin thread, and therefore the flow of thread from the bobbin, there is a tension screw on the bobbin case. To obtain a neat, flat stitch with the top thread but not the bobbin thread showing, turn the tension screw clockwise. This will tighten the tension and restrict the flow of the thread, so it won't show on the surface of the fabric. This is ideal for creating fine detail with the least amount of texture.

The amount of bobbin thread showing on the surface can be increased by tightening the tension of the top thread. Turn the dial or lever to a higher number or towards the plus sign. For a more exaggerated effect, loosen the bobbin tension too (turn the screw anticlockwise). This can be used to create a highly versatile, textured effect, which can be varied by changing the way you move the hoop and by setting your machine on either straight or zigzag stitch.

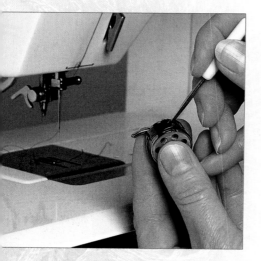

Turning the tension screw on the bobbin.

Binding the hoop

Before you start to embroider, bind the inner hoop with cotton tape. This will help it grip the fabric more effectively.

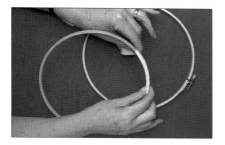

Binding the inner hoop.

Stretching the fabric in the hoop

When stretching your fabric in the hoop, it's important to have the fabric really taut as this prevents the stitches from puckering the fabric and allows the machine to stitch properly. Usually, if the machine appears to miss stitches, which will result in the thread breaking, it is due to the fabric not being stretched tightly enough.

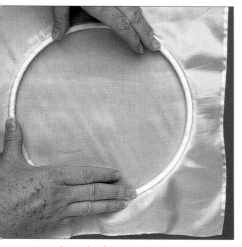

Stretching the fabric in the hoop.

Starting to embroider

Place your hoop under the machine. Remember that you will be working with the hoop 'upside down' so that the back of the fabric lies flat on the bed of the machine and the correct side of the picture is face up. Lower the presser bar to engage the top tension so that you don't create loops of thread on the back of your work.

For the best control of the hoop, rest your forearm or wrist on the table so that all the movement required to control the hoop is in the fingers. Think of the hoop as a pencil with which you are drawing. Keep your fingers on the hoop, safely out of the way of the needle, and move the hoop around under the needle. This will become more controlled with practice.

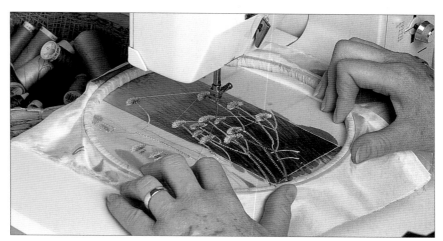

The correct way to hold the hoop under the machine.

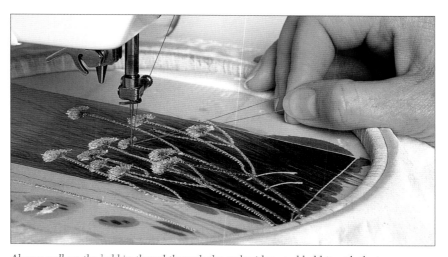

Always pull up the bobbin thread through the embroidery and hold it with the top thread to prevent them tangling. You can cut off these threads after you have worked a few stitches.

Silk painting

Understanding how paint behaves on silk is the key to successful silk painting, making best use of its strengths and working with its natural properties. My aim is to produce the same effect as a watercolour painting, though because of the way the paint behaves on the silk I have to adapt my technique. The basic principles are simple, and time spent practising will help you achieve the results you want.

On silk, paint will naturally spread across the surface, so you need to control it if you want to paint in detail. Drawing outlines with resist will contain the paint within a shape, but to paint detail within an area and stop it spreading too far needs a different approach.

Starting with the lightest colours first, I let each colour dry before applying the next. This helps to give more control to the flow of the paint; as each layer of colour is allowed to dry, the paint applied on top will spread less and less. This allows fine details to be painted (see 'Pots of Colour', page 22).

When painting fine detail it is essential to use small brushes. Experiment with different-sized brushes and see how far one brushstroke of paint will naturally travel across the fabric. Brush excess dye off your brush on the side of the palette for the finest painted line.

If we want areas of colour to blend with each other, both areas need to be damp. Wet the silk with a large brush and blot excess water with a paper towel. Colours should be mixed in the palette ready to be used so they can be applied quickly. I have found with experience that colours blend more successfully if you start with the palest tone and progress through to the darkest, overlapping each colour slightly.

For example, a field that shades to the palest tone towards the horizon should be painted from the horizon down to the stronger shades in the foreground, mixing all the colours needed in the palette before starting.

Scabious (Knautia arvensis)

The blended edges of the painted shapes, applied on to a damp background, give a sense of distance and project the embroidered flower forward. As in watercolour painting, start with the lightest colours and build up to the darkest.

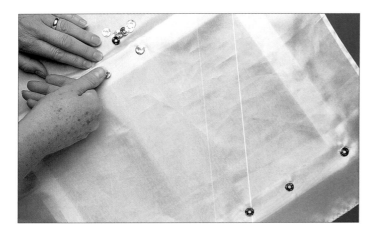

1. Begin by pinning the silk along one edge of the silk frame, making sure the fabric is straight. Pull the fabric firmly across the frame, and pin the opposite side. Finally, pin the two other sides. Space the pins approximately 8cm (3½in) apart. If you can see strong pull lines on the fabric connecting the pins, it is too tight. Release the two sides and restretch the fabric with a lighter touch.

2. Trace the elements of your design on to a sheet of acetate using a permanent marker. Here I intend to embroider the foreground flower and to paint all the other detail in the picture.

Tip

You may prefer to trace the image directly on to the silk from the photograph. Alternatively, you could draw the design on to the silk freehand.

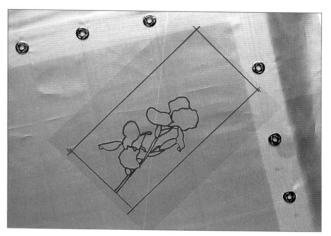

3. The completed design on acetate. This gives the shape and position of the embroidered area.

4. Place the acetate under your silk, preferably over a light box, and raise the image up so that it is touching the silk. If necessary, secure the acetate underneath with masking tape. Draw in a frame for your design using a ruler and air/water soluble pen, and then transfer the design. Refer to the photograph as you trace to make sure you are drawing accurately.

5. Remove the acetate. Using a pipette, go over the outline in resist. Make sure you draw a continuous line around each shape otherwise the paint will leak out of it. You can check that the line is complete by holding the image up to the light. While the resist is drying, start to mix your colours.

6. First mix the colours for the main petals. For a small area such as this, use a small brush (size 0). In this case, only one colour is needed – mid purple. Test the colour at the side of the picture if necessary before applying it to your picture.

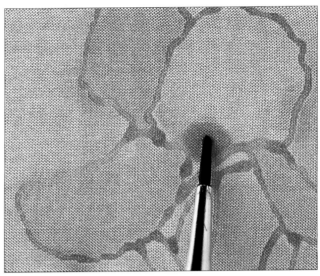

7. To apply a flat wash of colour, load the brush with paint, then rest it in the centre of the shape and allow the paint to spread to the edges.

8. Complete the flower, mixing up the appropriate colours as you need them. Select smaller brushes for painting small areas such as the stems. In this picture I have kept the painted flower simple as all the detail will be embroidered.

Tip

When applying paint to your background, avoid painting over the resist. Let the paint flow up to it.

Tip

To see the colours more clearly, place a sheet of white paper underneath the painted silk.

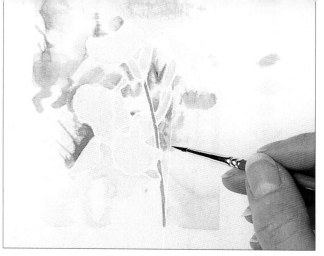

9. Mix all the colours that you need for the background and test them at the side of your picture (make sure you allow the colours to dry when testing them – they go paler as they dry). Starting with the lightest tones, begin to build up the background.

10. For small areas of colour, dab on the paint using a small paintbrush to prevent it from spreading too far. For larger areas, work quickly, and use light, feathery strokes. Allow adjacent colours to spread and blend naturally – if the paint starts to spread too far, dry it quickly with a hairdryer; if it doesn't spread enough, wait until it is completely dry and then dampen the area you are working on using a paintbrush and clear water. This will allow the colours to flow and blend more easily.

11. Carry on building up the background, continuously referring to the photograph to make sure the composition and colours are correct. Complete the background by applying the darkest tones last of all.

This is the completed background. The next stage is to press the silk with a hot iron for two minutes to fix the dye to the silk. Wash the silk in hot, soapy water to remove the resist, rinse in clean water, then iron it dry to avoid any creases in the fabric. You are now ready to embroider the flowers in the foreground.

Tip

To retain white areas, leave the silk bare, but don't outline them in resist otherwise you will get a hard edge – you will need to paint around them carefully with a small brush.

Starting to stitch

Machine embroidery can be fine and delicate and sit snugly on the fabric, or bold and textured with raised stitches standing proud and creating interest. Understanding the effect you want and how to achieve it is an important step in creating machine embroidered flowers.

There is a good reason why machine embroidery is sometimes called thread painting – it is the blending of coloured stitches in a painterly way to create the illusion of a landscape or garden. Stitches can vary in size, direction as well as colour, and though used in a similar way to brushstrokes of paint, they have the added advantage of texture, which catches the light and gives the work an extra dimension. Unlike painting, however, in which you move the paintbrush over your canvas, in machine embroidery you move your canvas (the hoop) under the paintbrush, which is equivalent to the needle of the machine.

Tension

Altering the tension on the machine is a way of adding more interest and texture to a technique. With freehand machine embroidery we are creating surface stitching, and therefore the two threads can be visible on the surface. This can be exaggerated by tightening the top tension and loosening the bobbin. This has the effect of pulling the bobbin thread through the fabric into loops.

Here I used dark green in the bobbin, mid green on top, and a spiralling straight stitch to create an overall texture for distant trees.

For the middle distance grass, I first created a foundation of mid and dark green vertical straight stitches. Then with pale green thread in the top and in the bobbin I worked longer, vertical stitches to highlight the blades of grass.

A series of zigzag stitches worked on the spot at an angle to the stem was used to create these ears of barley.

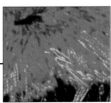

I used a wide zigzag stitch fanning out from the centre of the flower. The darkest shade was applied first and the mid tones added at the outer edge. Finally a few straight stitches were used, in the palest tone, to highlight the edge of each petal.

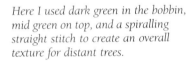

Stitch length

You are in control of the length of the stitches. The feed dog has been removed so that you are free to move the hoop in any direction, but this also means you can vary the length of stitch by altering the speed at which you move the hoop. If you move your hands slowly you will get small stitches; if you move your hands quickly the stitches will be larger. Try to keep the speed of the machine constant so that varying the speed at which you move your hands will alter the length of stitch in a more predictable way.

These simple techniques are the building blocks you will use as a base for your embroideries. Practising them will build up your experience, eye–hand coordination and confidence. The following exercises will introduce you to the basic idea of painting with the sewing machine.

Straight stitch

Practise a neat, flat stitch with only the top thread showing. It gives a smooth appearance, creating the least texture. If the bobbin thread is visible, tighten the bobbin tension a little by turning the screw clockwise. This will keep the bobbin thread on the back of the work.

For a different effect, try threading up the machine with two different colours so you can see the effects of altered tension. This method creates texture and, by tightening the top tension (higher number or towards the plus sign), enables the two thread colours to show on the surface and helps you to blend colours more easily. For maximum effect, tighten the top tension even more to pull the bobbin thread up in loops. If the top thread breaks, loosen the bobbin tension (turn screw anticlockwise) to achieve the same result.

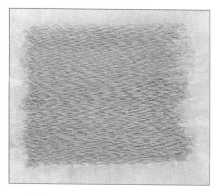

Parallel straight lines: a flat filling-in stitch, achieved by moving the hoop backwards and forwards at a steady speed to produce stitches of a consistent size.

Parallel curved line: produced in the same way as parallel straight lines, to follow the contour of a shape.

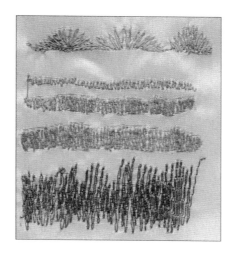

A jagged stitch could be worked horizontally, diagonally or vertically to produce texture with a well-defined direction. Created by moving the hoop quickly, backwards and forwards, for a short distance.

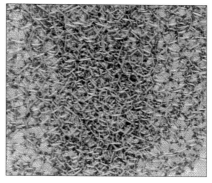

Small spiralling hand movement creates a small-scale textured effect with stitches lying in all different directions. The darkest shade is in the bobbin and pulled to the surface by a tight top tension.

Zigzag stitch

This in essence gives a broad line with which to draw. It can be smooth or textured, worked in small broken marks or a continual line.
Remember that all the exercises below can be done with altered tensions to add texture and help blend colours.

Held on the spot to create raised dots of colour. These can be varied in size; the longer the fabric is held on the spot, the more raised the stitches become. You can also alter the direction in which they lie by rotating the hoop.

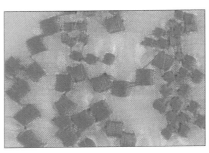

Slow movement forwards or backwards, for a short distance, to create a block of colour. Move the hoop fractionally and repeat. To change the angle of a block, rotate the hoop.

Slight movement sideways to elongate the shape, using the widest zigzag setting. This example used a tighter top tension to reveal the darker bobbin thread.

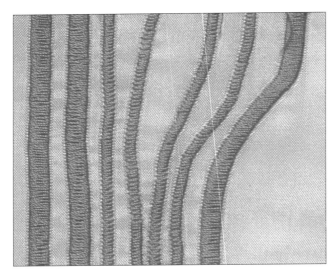

Slow movement forwards or backwards, for a long distance, to create columns of colour. This can be in a straight line or curved.

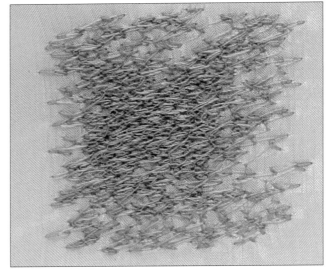

Compact, random movements to create overall texture. This shows a darker colour pulled up from the bobbin by a tighter top tension.

Zigzag stitch, altering the width

This involves moving the hoop with one hand and changing the width of zigzag stitch with the other. Use slow hand movements, forwards or backwards, increasing and decreasing the width control, to 'draw' shapes with a varying width of line. This requires a little practice – if spaces appear between the stitches, move the hoop more slowly. Every machine has a width-of-stitch control for the zigzag stitch, and this is usually selected before you start to sew.

Each of the techniques shown below can be tried with a tighter top tension (or looser bobbin tension) so that the bobbin colour shows on the surface of the embroidery too. This has the effect of giving each shape a shadow or a three-dimensional appearance.

Moving the hoop slowly, quickly increase from zero setting (straight stitch) to the widest setting and back again to create a short, rounded shape.

Moving the hoop slowly, gradually increase the width of stitch control from zero to the widest setting and back again to create a long, narrow shape. Notice the darker shade from the bobbin is visible at the edge of each shape.

Moving the hoop slowly, decrease from the widest setting (highest number) to zero/straight stitch. This can be worked in a curve or a straight line.

Grouping flowers and foliage by technique

You can group flowers into types based on their shape or construction, and once a hand movement or technique is mastered for one flower in that group it can be modified slightly and the colours changed to create another. For example, similar techniques can be used for peonies, roses, hydrangeas and rhododendrons. With a change of colour and overall shape, the technique for a laburnum flower is repeated for a delphinium. The list below groups flowers and foliage according to common techniques. These have been divided into two categories, straight stitch and zigzag.

Straight stitch techniques

For plumes of grasses and foliage for flowers, use a jagged straight stitch worked in a column up one side, then down the other in a straight line or a curve.

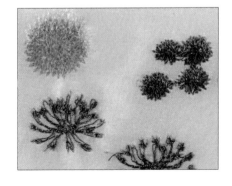

Alliums, agapanthus, globe thistles and echinops all share characteristics – use a spiky straight stitch radiating out from a central point.

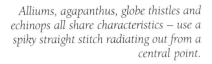

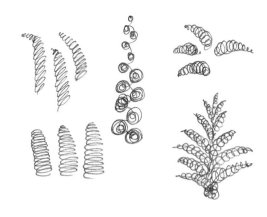

Distant delphiniums, lupins, foxgloves, hollyhocks, buddleia, ligularia, lilac (syringa) and foreground astilbe are created using spiralling columns of straight stitch.

Large, multi-petalled flowers such as roses, peonies and clematis, in the distance, created with a small, spiralling straight stitch, starting in the centre and making larger stitches towards the outside of the flower.

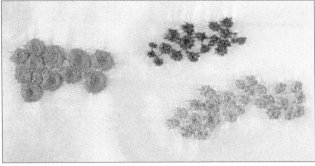

Large-petalled flowers such as iris, poppy and hibiscus, in the foreground, should be treated in the same way as broad-shaped leaves. Use parallel rows of straight stitch following the shape of the petals. Subtle colour changes and shading can be handled with this technique.

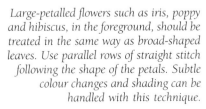

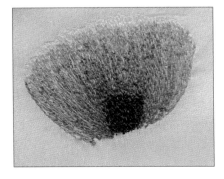

Broad, lance-shaped leaves such as laurel, rhododendron, hosta and foxglove, in the foreground, produced using parallel rows of straight stitch following the contours of the leaves. This will allow shading with a tonal range of threads.

Long strap-like leaf shapes, found with irises, phormium and gladioli, produced by parallel rows of straight stitch, closely worked.

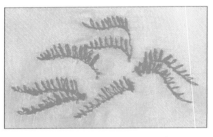

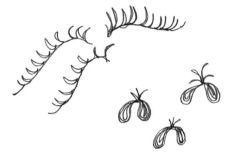

For middle-distance crocosmia and irises, use straight stitch drawing along the shape of the flower.

Zigzag stitch techniques

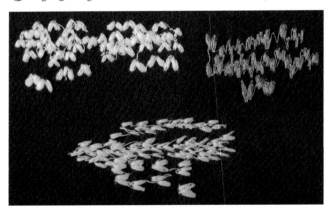

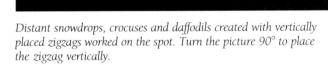

Distant snowdrops, crocuses and daffodils created with vertically placed zigzags worked on the spot. Turn the picture 90° to place the zigzag vertically.

Middle-distance daffodils and foreground snowdrops and crocuses created with V-shaped sets of zigzags.

Mound-forming plants with small-headed flowers such as lobelia, santolina, potentilla and aubretia are created with small zigzags worked on the spot in a curved shape. Slowly rotate the hoop a little to place the zigzags at the right angle.

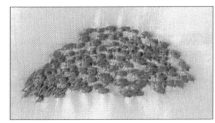

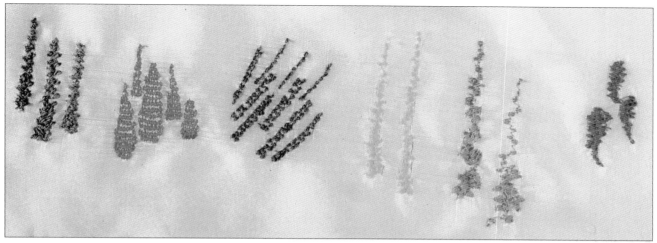

Lupins

Delphiniums

Lavender

Verbascum

Tall, narrow flowers are created using small zigzags worked on the spot and grouped together in various ways to create different shapes.

Hollyhocks

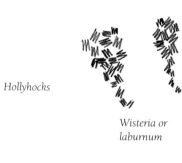

Wisteria or laburnum

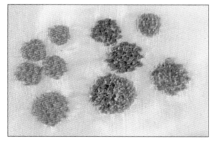

Round-headed flowers, such as phlox, hydrangea, azalea, peony, euphorbia and rhododendron, are worked in clusters of small zigzags on the spot, all facing different directions. This is achieved by altering the angle of the hoop.

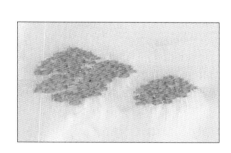

Achillea

Flat-headed flowers such as achillea, cow parsley and sedum – use small zigzags worked in horizontal clusters.

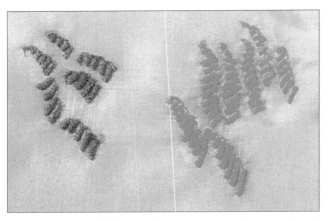

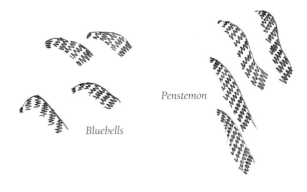

Penstemon

Bluebells

Tubular, bell-shaped flowers such as penstemon, distant foxgloves, bluebells, crocosmia, campanula and nicotiana are created using narrow columns of closely worked zigzags in diagonal parallel lines.

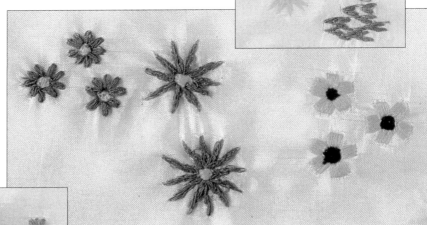

For star-like flowers, for example wild garlic, asters, anemone, oxeye daisy, Magnolia stellata and jasmine, use zigzag stitch rotated around a central point. With the needle in the centre of the flower, rotate the hoop a few degrees and work zigzag on the spot. Repeat until the flower is completed. Finally add a small zigzag in the centre.

Foxgloves

This is created by altering the width of zigzag along the length of each trumpet. Straight stitch up the central stem and down a trumpet, zigzag back to the stem and repeat, increasing the size of the trumpets towards the base of the flower.

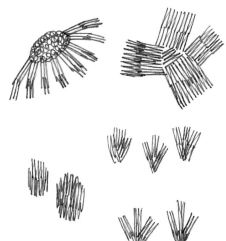

For larger flower heads in the foreground of a picture, use a double row of zigzag, for example tulips, crocuses, poppies and daisies. A spiralling straight stitch works well for the centres.

Pointed leaves are made by slowly increasing and decreasing the width of the zigzag to draw the shape. Take a straight stitch out to the end of each leaf and zigzag back along it to the stem. Work down one side and then the other.

For long, strap-like leaf shapes in the foreground, use closely worked zigzag with the width decreasing along its length. Leaves can be made as large as necessary with this method by laying several lines of zigzag side-by-side.

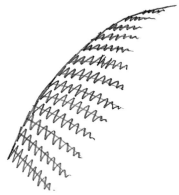

Ferns in the foreground are created with openly worked zigzag with the width changing along the length of the fronds. Start with the stem and work straight stitch out from it, then zigzag back to the stem increasing the width of the zigzag as you go.

For broad, lance-shaped leaves such as laurel, rhododendron, hosta and foxglove, in the middle distance or foreground, use closely worked zigzag with the width increasing and decreasing along its length. A double row of zigzag will give more width to the leaves and echo their natural form. Angle the hoop so the zigzag sits diagonally within the leaf shape.

For broad, lance-shaped leaves such as laurel and rhododendron, in the middle distance, use zigzag worked on the spot in various sizes, lying in different directions.

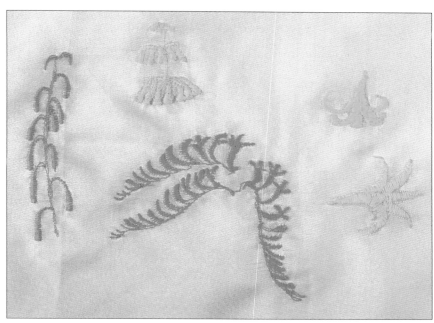

Rounded leaves are created by quickly increasing and decreasing the width of the zigzag to draw the shape.

Trumpet-shaped flowers, such as day lilies, crocosmia and Candelabra primula, are created using closely worked zigzag, decreasing in width towards the flower stem, moving the hoop in a curved line. Work straight stitch out from the stem, and zigzag back.

Combining techniques

Foreground French lavender, created using two techniques combined – a V-shaped pair of zigzag stitches and a short column of spiralling straight stitch.

Foreground daffodils formed with a column of zigzag for the trumpet and V-shaped zigzags for the petals. The deeper shade of yellow is pulled up from the bobbin with a tight top tension.

Leaves with serrated edges, for example holly. First, zigzags are worked on the spot with the needle placed on the outer edge of the leaf. Next, a column of zigzag is worked down one half of the leaf, increasing in width at the centre. Finally, this is repeated down the other side of the leaf.

A combination of curved straight stitch was used to form the basic shape of the allium or agapanthus flower heads, with star-like flowers worked in zigzags fanning out from the centre.

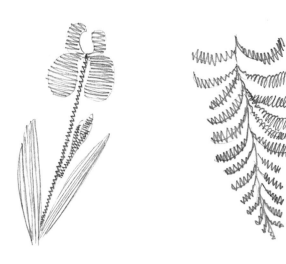

For foreground irises and wisteria, increase and decrease the width of zigzag along the petals. Combine this with parallel rows of straight stitch for iris stems. Notice the colour changes within the wisteria. Try this in shades of yellow for laburnum flowers.

In this picture, the negatives have begun to be put in around the leaf and flower shapes. The technique used to do this depends on the background and the amount of texture needed. This dark stitching will make the light colour in the foxglove stand out and form a strong basis for the foreground embroidery.

Thinking in stitch

The art of translating a design into stitch is the ability to 'think in stitches'. It depends on understanding the different techniques available to you and how they can be used together, with the right colour combinations, to achieve various textures and effects. The following project was based on a series of photographs taken of a show garden at Hampton Court Flower Show.

The two photographs shown on the left were overlapped to create a continuous vista of flowers and foliage. This was then translated into the painted background shown at the top of the next page.

On the painted background, the white lines show where resist has been used to mark the positions of flower heads or to outline areas of foliage. The bamboo fence in the background and the wooden borders of the flower bed in the foreground will remain as painted areas. A simple wash of green is sufficient as a background colour for the foliage. Small areas of colour such as flower heads will be put in with stitch and do not need to be painted at this stage.

The sketch map of stitch techniques shown below can also be used to record the colours of thread chosen for each area. You could also note down which colour to use in the bobbin and which should go in the top of the machine as decisions are made. Remember to always choose threads in natural light.

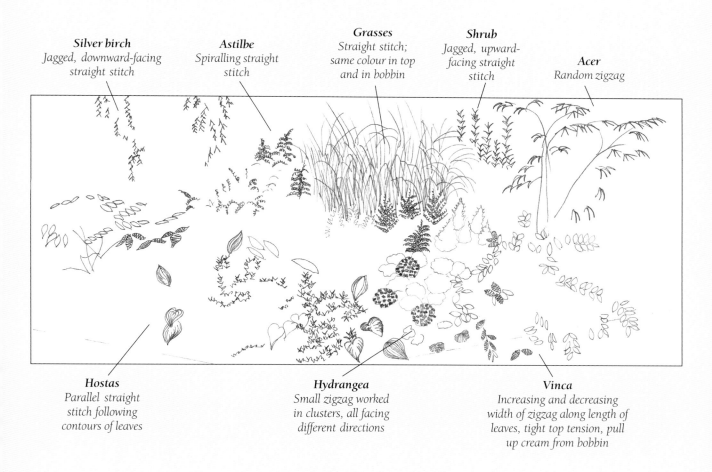

Silver birch
Jagged, downward-facing straight stitch

Astilbe
Spiralling straight stitch

Grasses
Straight stitch; same colour in top and in bobbin

Shrub
Jagged, upward-facing straight stitch

Acer
Random zigzag

Hostas
Parallel straight stitch following contours of leaves

Hydrangea
Small zigzag worked in clusters, all facing different directions

Vinca
Increasing and decreasing width of zigzag along length of leaves, tight top tension, pull up cream from bobbin

Eryngiums and Daisies

The design for the cover of this book was derived from a number of photographs that I took of yellow daisies and purple eryngiums. I liked the dramatic effect created by the bright, complementary colours of these two flowers, which when put together as a composition made a stunning design for the book.

With the flowers at the front of the photographs sharply in focus and the smaller, more distant flowers blurred, the idea emerged to embroider the foreground flowers, covering the bottom two-thirds of the design, and to paint the out-of-focus background, adding depth to the composition.

I began by cutting and pasting flowers from a series of enlarged colour photocopies of my source photographs (shown on the right) to create the design. I favoured the composition in the top photograph but wanted stronger colours in the foreground for contrast and more interest.

I then transferred the design to the silk, and outlined the foreground flowers using resist to mark their positions ready for embroidering. The rest of the silk was painted using tones of purple and yellow to give a strong, fully painted backdrop. I worked while the fabric was still damp, allowing colours to merge and create an out-of-focus effect which adds to the sense of depth.

The finished embroidery

The centres of the eryngiums were created with small zigzags worked on the spot in a series of curved lines using shades of purple. They were then encircled with straight stitch in a dark shade of purple to further isolate and define them.

For the spiky petals of the eryngiums, I used straight stitch in various shades of purple. They were formed by first working round the shape of each petal and then filling it in.

A spiralling straight stitch with two shades of orange was used to create the centres of the daisies. The petals are each embroidered using a wide zigzag worked horizontally along their length.

Using a small straight stitch and a loose bobbin tension, and with dark green on the top and orange in the bobbin, small loops of bobbin thread were pulled through to the surface, producing the flecked effect around the edge of these small, yellow flowers.

The Azalea Walk

The painted grass pathway leads your eye into the
picture and contrasts with the rich detail of the
embroidered areas.

Astilbes and Hostas

Created entirely with straight stitch, this embroidery
shows how versatile this stitch can be.

Daisies and Grasses

The softly painted background blends well with the richly embroidered foreground detail.

Pot and Pebbles

Astilbe

Using the various flower techniques described on pages 37 and 41, this project produces a small cluster of flowers based on a source photograph. The embroidery has a plain, unpainted background and is therefore an ideal starting point for the beginner.

Start by making a pencil sketch of the arrangement, or trace the flowers on to tracing paper or acetate. Alternatively you can draw them straight on to the silk.

You will need

Source photograph
Paper and pencil
Tracing paper or acetate
Permanent marker for tracing
Air/water soluble pen
White medium-weight silk
Bound 20cm (8in) embroidery hoop
Selection of coloured threads
Scissors

Source photograph. The astilbe are clearly defined, making the observation of shapes and decisions about which techniques to use easier. My initial sketch groups the flowers and their foliage together to create a simple composition.

1. Begin by gathering together your threads and the photograph on which you have based your design. Use this to check colours, texture and composition as you embroider. Stretch the silk in a bound hoop and place it over your pencil sketch or tracing, with the flat side downwards.

2. Trace over the pencil outline using an air/water soluble pen. Follow the central stem of each flower and leaf as a guide. This will be easier if you are able to work on a light box.

Tip

Keep the drawing as simple as possible – you only need guide lines. Refer to the photograph for detail.

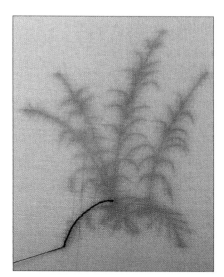

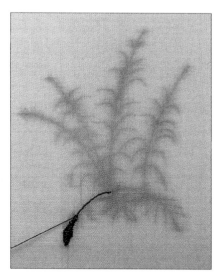

3. Start with the leaves. Use the same green in the top of the machine and in the bobbin, and set the tension to normal. Sew along the central vein of a frond using straight stitch, working from the centre of the plant outwards to the tip of the frond.

4. Work back along the straight stitch and embroider the small leaves growing from the central vein. Gradually increase the width of the stitch and then decrease it to form the shape of each leaf.

5. Complete all the leaves and fronds in the same way – straight stitch to the end of a leaf, then zigzag back along it. Trim off the threads.

6. Now begin the flowers. Thread the top of the machine and the bobbin with the burgundy-coloured thread. Set the tension to normal, and put in the flower stems using straight stitch. Start at the top of the left-hand flower and carry the thread across from one flower to the next.

7. Snip the threads that have been carried over, as close as possible to the fabric. Snip the threads on the back of the embroidery as well or they will be visible through the silk.

8. Identify the darkest parts of the flowers in the photograph, and embroider these using dark pink in the top of the machine and in the bobbin. Set the tension to normal. Embroider a line of straight stitch from the central stem to the tip of each flower segment, and then spiral back along it.

9. Working from flower to flower along each stem, complete the lower, dark-toned parts of the flowers, and then trim off the threads.

10. Blend the dark pink with the mid tone by leaving the dark pink thread in the bobbin and threading the top of the machine with the mid-tone pink. Tighten the top tension until the bobbin colour is visible. Embroider the mid-toned parts of the flowers, overlapping some of the dark-toned stitches and working higher up the stems.

Tip

In embroidery, always start with the darkest tones and end with the lightest. The darkest parts of a plant tend to be at the back of the plant and at the base, depending on the light source. The lightest parts tend to be at the top and outer edges. Turn the photograph upside down to help you identify colour and shape.

11. Now introduce the lightest tone of pink. Thread the bobbin with the mid tone, and the top of the machine with the light pink thread. Make sure the bobbin colour is visible. Embroider the lighter areas of the flowers. You may need to move from one part of the plant to another with this colour. Snip off the threads that have been carried over.

12. Complete the flowers by embroidering the lightest parts using the light pink thread in the top of the machine and in the bobbin.

Tip

When you have finished an embroidery, look at your composition and correct any imbalances. I have added an extra flower on the right-hand side of the picture so that it is better balanced. Three or five flowers often work better in a design than two or four.

Astilbes

All of the embroideries below follow a similar style to the astilbes. The simple pencil sketches help me design the composition, then I use the source photographs for detailed reference.

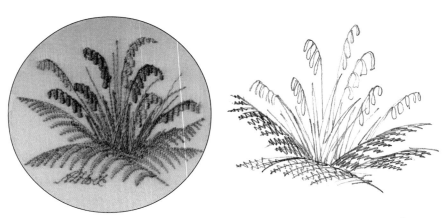

Using a darker tone in the bobbin for the bluebells gives a shaded effect and makes them look more three-dimensional.

Two different shades of purple are used for the irises. The palest tone in the bobbin when pulled to the surface with a tight top tension creates a highlight.

These foxgloves are a good example of 'drawing' with a varying width of zigzag for the flowers and leaves. Complete the trumpets first and then embroider the stem with a narrow zigzag.

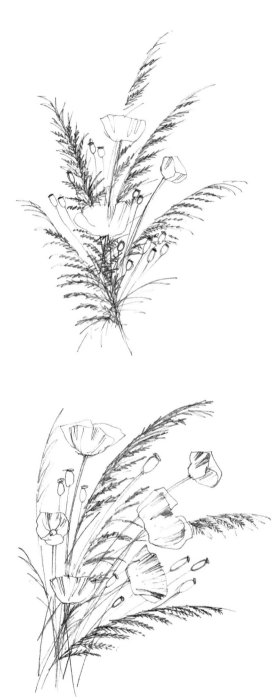

The grasses in this composition are worked in straight stitch with a loose bobbin tension and tight top tension, so the darker thread is pulled to the surface. The poppies are bands of zigzag filling the petal shapes and the poppy seed heads are small zigzag stitches closely worked in a short column.

Delphiniums

In this project you will embroider a foreground flower in detail, and have a painted background suggesting more of the same flower receding into the distance. The source photograph shows a single flower in detail – use this for reference, and make a pencil sketch to compose the rest of the picture. Trace your design on to tracing paper or acetate ready to transfer on to the silk, or if you are sufficiently confident, draw the design straight on to the silk freehand.

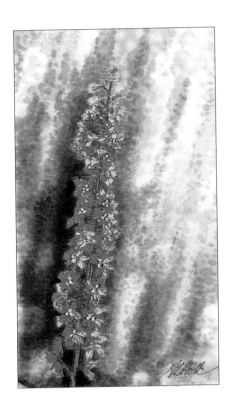

To create my composition, I took my source photograph, and replaced the background foliage with more delphiniums receding into the background. These I decided to paint on rather than stitch, leaving the foreground delphinium the only embroidered element in the picture.

You will need

Resist in a pipette with a nib
Source photograph
Paper and pencil
Ruler
Tracing paper or acetate
Permanent marker for tracing
Air/water soluble pen
White medium-weight silk
Silk frame, 30 x 25cm (12 x 10in)
Approximately 20 silk pins
Silk paints
Small paintbrush
Mixing palette
Bound 20cm (8in)
embroidery hoop
Selection of coloured threads
Liquid soap
Iron

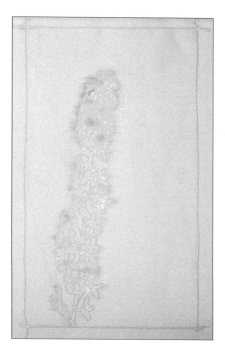

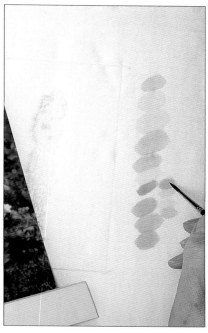

1. Pin your silk to a silk frame and draw in the rectangular frame for your design using a ruler and an air/water soluble pen. Trace the outline for the design on to the silk by placing your pencil drawing or tracing underneath it. If possible, do this over a light box. Use the photograph for reference.

2. Take away the pencil drawing, then outline the flower shapes in resist. Apply the resist using a pipette. Also outline the rectangular border in order to contain the paint.

3. Using the silk paints, mix a range of blues, purples, greens and pinks. Test the colours on the silk, outside the border. Remember to let them dry. Use your photograph for reference.

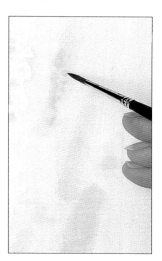

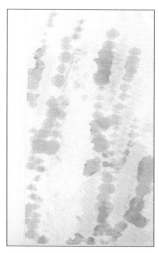

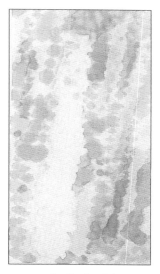

4. Referring to the photograph and your drawing, apply the paint to the silk. Use the brush to dab on the colour, and allow it to spread and blend naturally.

5. Gradually build up the colour, starting with the lightest tones and ending with the darkest. If the dyes dry on the fabric they will not blend, so dampen the whole picture with clean water and then paint on to it quickly where you want the colours to merge.

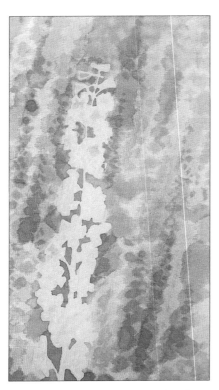

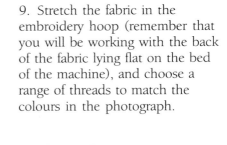

7. Apply dark blue to the inside of each flower. Load a small brush with paint, then hold the brush inside the flower until the paint has spread to fill the shape.

6. Put in some dark areas both around and within the flower to emphasise the edges of the resist.

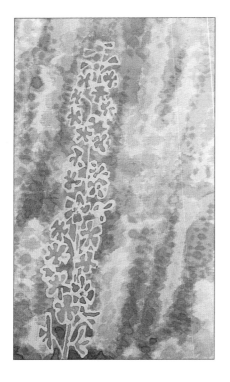

8. Wait for the paint to dry, then iron the fabric for two minutes to fix the dye. Wash the silk in hot, soapy water to remove the resist, rinse in clear water, then iron your work dry to avoid creasing. You are now ready to start your embroidery.

9. Stretch the fabric in the embroidery hoop (remember that you will be working with the back of the fabric lying flat on the bed of the machine), and choose a range of threads to match the colours in the photograph.

60

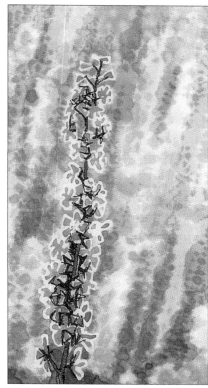

Tip

Before you start sewing, roll up the sides of the silk and pin them in place to avoid accidentally sewing them to the back of your embroidery.

10. Start at the back of the flower head, with the petals that are in shadow. Choose the two darkest shades of purple, and use one in the bobbin and the other in the top of the machine. 'Draw in' the negative shapes between the flowers using straight stitch. Trim the connecting threads.

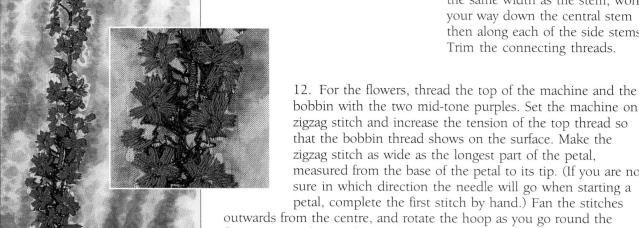

Tip

Using two colours at a time adds interest to a picture, and gives it more depth.

11. For the stems, thread the bobbin with the darker green, and the top of the machine with the lighter green. Tighten the top tension a little so that you can see the bobbin thread more clearly. Using narrow zigzag stitch, set to the same width as the stem, work your way down the central stem then along each of the side stems. Trim the connecting threads.

12. For the flowers, thread the top of the machine and the bobbin with the two mid-tone purples. Set the machine on zigzag stitch and increase the tension of the top thread so that the bobbin thread shows on the surface. Make the zigzag stitch as wide as the longest part of the petal, measured from the base of the petal to its tip. (If you are not sure in which direction the needle will go when starting a petal, complete the first stitch by hand.) Fan the stitches outwards from the centre, and rotate the hoop as you go round the flower. Remember to change the width of the zigzag according to the size of the petal you are embroidering, and be careful not to sew over the dark purple stitching you did earlier.

Tip

When your machine is threaded up with two different colours, sew everything you can see in the photograph that requires that colour combination before moving on to the next. This will keep the amount of re-threading to a minimum.

13. Leave the bobbin colour the same, and thread the top of the machine with the lightest tone of purple. Pick out the palest parts of the flower and put in the highlights using zigzag stitch. You may need to sew over some of your previous stitching to link the colours together.

14. Thread the top of the machine with the same mid-tone purple that is in the bobbin, and run through the highlights using straight stitch to blend them in with the other colours. Trim off any connecting threads.

15. To embroider the flower centres, use the darkest purple tone in the bobbin and the off-white in the top of the machine. Set the top tension slightly tighter than normal so that the bobbin colour is visible. Sew three small zigzags in the centre of each flower – one for each of the tiny petals. Snip off the connecting threads.

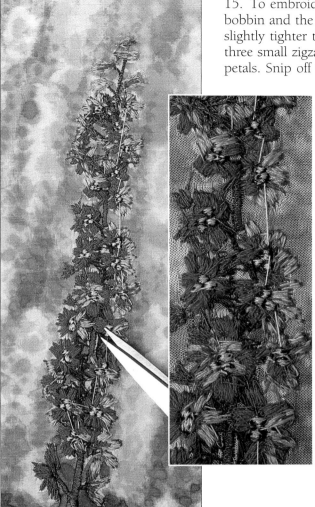

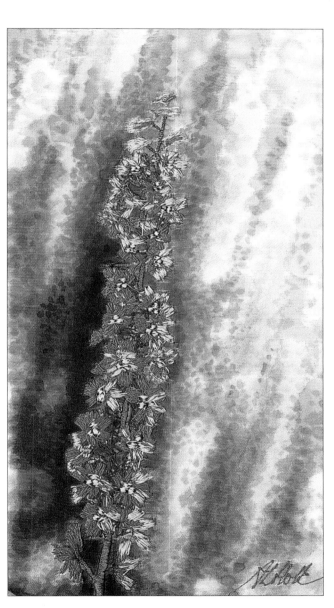

Delphiniums

When I had completed this embroidery, I decided to strengthen the painted background in order to create more tonal contrast between the background and the embroidered delphinium to make it stand out more.

Tip

When reaching the final stages of your embroidery, compare it with your source photograph and sketches to assess whether you have achieved the desired end result. Check the balance of the composition in terms of colour, shape and tone and adjust it if necessary. For example, are the dark areas dark enough? Are the colours strong or light enough?

Verbascum

The evening light has back lit this verbascum, creating a strong highlight around the petals and buds. This was recreated by pulling an off-white thread in the bobbin to the surface with a tight top tension, and painting the background in strong colours to emphasise the highlight.

Salvia pratensis

Parallel rows of straight stitch for the stems in shades of purple and
green were completed before the more complicated 'drawing' of the
petal shapes.

Alliums and Tulips

This is a more complex embroidery, needing different skills for each flower and its foliage, and an understanding of how the various elements of the picture fit together to form a coherent design. In this project you will work directly from the source photograph.

You will need

Resist in a pipette with a nib
Source photograph
Paper and pencil
Ruler
Tracing paper
Permanent marker for tracing
Air/water soluble pen
White medium-weight silk
Silk frame, 30 x 25cm
(12 x 10in)
Approximately 20 silk pins
Silk paints
Small paintbrushes
Mixing palette
Bound 20cm (8in) embroidery
hoop
Selection of coloured threads
Liquid soap
Iron

The source photograph was cropped and only the middle section used for the composition. I then made a sketch showing the various types of foliage and flower shapes, and made notes on which stitches to use for each plant. I decided to use a jagged straight stitch for the background foliage, a spiralling straight stitch with loose bobbin tension for the roses, three parallel blocks of zigzag for the tulip heads and parallel straight stitch for the leaves, blocks of zigzag at various angles for the foreground foliage, spiralling straight stitch in a column for the tall, purple veronica in the foreground, and spiralling straight stitch worked in a spherical shape for the alliums.

1. Begin by pinning the silk to the frame. Place the photograph underneath the silk on a raised surface, so that it is as close to the silk as possible. First draw in a frame for your design using a ruler and the air/water soluble pen, and then draw in the key elements of the design. Work over a light box if possible. Trace the picture on to tracing paper or acetate if the detail is not visible through the silk.

2. Remove the photograph from underneath the silk and, using the traced elements as a guide, draw in the smaller shapes by eye, using the photograph for reference.

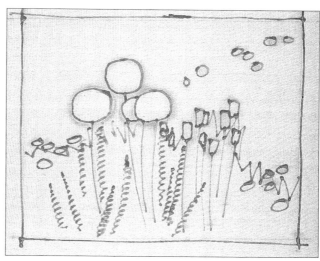

3. Outline the main elements (flower heads and stems) in resist applied using a pipette and nib. Put a line of resist across the picture to mark where the foreground foliage ends and the background begins. Simplify the composition by leaving out any unnecessary detail, such as the tree trunk.

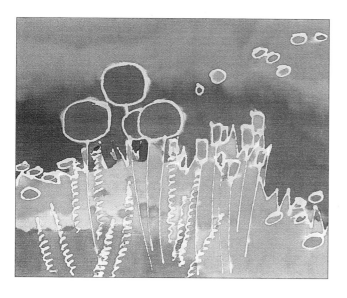

Tip

If you intend to cover the whole of your background with embroidery, you just need a wash of background colour on which to place your stitches.

4. Paint the background using a simple wash of dark and mid green. Let the colour flood up to the lines of resist, but avoid painting over them. Remember this is just the background colour – all the detail will be embroidered.

5. Choose your threads, matching the colours to the photograph. Choose three or four shades for each type of flower, and five or six for the foliage. Select a broad tonal range, from the darkest colour you can identify in the photograph to the lightest. This will make your embroidery more three dimensional; a narrow tonal range results in a 'flat' image.

6. Iron and wash your fabric (see page 31), and stretch it tightly in an embroidery hoop. Thread the top of the machine and the bobbin with the darkest green thread, and set the tension to normal. Identify all the dark green areas (the 'negative shapes') in the photograph, and fill them in using straight stitch, echoing the directions and sizes of the leaves. A jagged short stitch will work well for the background, and use long, straight stitches between the iris leaves, for example.

7. Leave the dark green in the bobbin and thread the top of the machine with the next lighter shade of green. Make sure you can see the bobbin threads by tightening the top tension. Start putting in the leaf shapes within the dark green area of the background, and extending a little way above it. Use straight stitch worked backwards and forwards to create tiny blocks of colour. In the upper part of the picture, work up and down in a random motion to create the impression of foliage in the distance.

Tip

To help you identify the darkest areas in a photograph, try turning it upside down – this helps you see shape and tone, without the distraction of content.

Tip

Keep the background foliage simple, creating only the *impression* of foliage, with no unnecessary detail. This creates a good basis for the foreground flowers.

8. Move the top colour to the bobbin, and thread the top of the machine with the next lighter shade of green. Using the same technique as before, embroider the lighter areas of the picture, overlapping some of the previous stitching and taking it higher up. Trim any connecting threads if you move from one area to another.

Tip

Remember that you are gradually moving from the darkest to the lightest tones, introducing one new thread at a time so a blending effect is achieved.

9. Thread the bobbin with the mid-purple tone, and leave the lighter shade of green in the top of the machine. Create tiny areas of straight stitch sewn in a spiral – the purple in the bobbin will appear as small dots of colour, giving the impression of distant flowers.

69

10. For the pale roses in the top right of the picture, use pale pink on the top of the machine and deep pink in the bobbin. Tighten the top tension so that a lot of the bobbin thread shows through. Work straight stitch in a spiral motion from the centre of each rose outwards. Snip any connecting threads between the roses close to the surface of your work.

11. Use the same technique for the darker roses, threading the bobbin with burgundy, and using the mid-tone pink in the top of the machine. For an even darker effect, use dark pink in the bobbin and in the top of the machine. Create a series of roses in various colours and sizes across the picture.

12. For the foreground leaves, use a different set of greens from the background foliage. Use the darkest green in the bobbin, and a mid green in the top of the machine. Make sure the bobbin thread is showing through by tightening the top tension. Using zigzag stitch, work a series of parallel, diagonal stitches across the picture, first in one direction and then in the other to create an impression of leaves.

13. Put in the mid-tone foliage. Put the top colour in the bobbin, and replace the top thread with one a shade lighter. Using the same technique, embroider within and around the previously stitched leaves, taking your stitching higher up the foreground foliage.

14. Put the top colour in the bobbin, and thread the top of the machine with the next shade lighter. Use the same technique to complete the lighter areas of the foreground foliage. Keep referring to the source photograph to identify the detail.

15. Leave the bobbin thread the same and thread the top of the machine with the lightest shade of green. Set the machine on straight stitch, and put in the highlights using sharp, jagged stitches. These will be mainly at the top of the foreground foliage, contrasting well with the dark base of the background and making the foreground stand out.

16. For the dark areas at the base of the allium heads, thread the bobbin with the deepest shade of lilac, and the top of the machine with a shade lighter. Tighten the top tension so that the bobbin thread shows through, and work straight stitch in tight spirals – this technique creates small star shapes that resemble the individual flowers on the allium heads.

17. Leave the same colour in the top of the machine, and thread the bobbin with the next shade lighter. Using the same technique, embroider the lighter areas of the alliums. Work your way further up the flowers, partly overlapping the previous stitches.

18. For the lightest areas of the alliums, put off-white in the bobbin and the palest lilac in the top of the machine. Work the highlights at the very top of the flower heads.

19. Replace the off-white in the bobbin with the lightest shade of lilac and blend the highlights with the darker parts of the flower heads by stitching over a small part of each.

72

20. For the tulip heads, use off-white in the bobbin and cream in the top of the machine. Fill the tulip heads using wide zigzag stitch, giving each flower three petal tips and a rounded base. You will need to work with your design turned sideways.

21. For the sepals, rotate the picture sideways again and sew narrow bands of small zigzag stitches at the base of each flower. Set the tension to normal. Keep off-white in the bobbin, and use the second lightest shade of blue-green in the top of the machine.

22. Next embroider the tall, purple flowers. Use dark purple in the bobbin and a mid purple in the top of the machine. Tighten the top tension so that both threads show, and work a straight stitch up the centre of each flower then spiral back down.

23. Add a highlight down the left-hand side of the purple flower spikes using the same technique. Keep the same colour in the bobbin (this helps the highlight to blend in), and put a paler purple in the top of the machine.

24. Moving now to the tulip leaves in the bottom right-hand corner of the picture, thread the bobbin with the darkest green and the top of the machine with the next shade lighter. Turn your work sideways on and embroider the darkest parts of the leaves using wide zigzag stitch. Move the hoop slowly to keep the stitches closely worked.

25. Repeat this technique higher up the leaves, using the colour from the top of the machine in the bobbin and a shade lighter in the top of the machine.

26. Move the top colour to the bobbin, and replace it with a lighter shade of green. Put in the highlights on the tips of the leaves and the tulip stems. Use fairly long straight stitch so that they stand out against the background.

Tip

If you are adding a highlight, break it up by putting a darker tone in the bobbin, otherwise it will be too strong.

Alliums and Tulips

I assessed the embroidery at the final stage and added some more roses in the foreground on the right-hand side to balance up the distribution of colour. I used pale pink in the top of the machine and deep pink in the bobbin. I added a few selected highlights to the tulip leaves using the same light green in the top of the machine and the bobbin, and then cut the connecting threads.

Blue Irises

The iris leaves are embroidered using parallel lines of straight stitch, closely observing how the colours change, working from the darkest tones through to the lightest.

Silver Birch

Closely worked columns of zigzag are used for the tree trunks. A straight stitch spiralled from the centre of each flower creates the roses.

The White Bench

The white bench, which has a painted seat and stitched ironwork, sits on an embroidered background of greens and whites. The white roses are worked with a spiralling straight stitch and the hydrangeas consist of clusters of small zigzags.

Pinks and Lavenders

The leaves in the pot are embroidered by increasing and decreasing the width of zigzag along the length of each leaf. The lavender flowers use a combination of techniques – a spiky straight stitch for the top part of the flower and a compact, spiralled straight stitch for the base. The pinks in the foreground are small zigzag stitches worked from the centre of the flower outwards. The centres are then completed with a small circle of deep pink worked in straight stitch.

Alliums and Irises

Notice the long stitches used in the foreground grasses. They stand out from the background and add depth to

How to present your finished embroidery

An embroidery needs to be stretched and mounted to keep it flat and taut. Ideally, it should be framed and put under glass to protect it from dust. It needs to be well presented using acid-free card and mounts that complement the work. Always ensure you allow enough material around the edge of your embroidery for folding round the mount board.

   Mounts and frames should enhance your embroidery, focus the eye on the work and not overpower it. Choose a mount whose colour works well with your embroidery. Consider also the width of the card margin relative to the embroidery/window size. Do you feel it is too tight or too broad a margin? Get to know which style of mount you prefer. Any good framer will be able to guide you through the choosing of mounts and frames, but it can be helpful if you have ideas of your own, based on your personal style.

How to stretch and mount your work

You will need

For lacing the finished work:

Acid-free mount board, cut to size
(it should be slightly larger than
your embroidery)

Large-eyed needle

Perle cotton, linen thread or any
strong equivalent thread

Dressmaking pins to position
work on to board

**For framing (if you choose to
frame your work yourself):**

Acid-free mounts in toning and
matching colours

Suitable frames and backing board

Glass

Screw eyes or d-rings

Strong nylon cord

Framing gun to pin frame, glass
and board together

1. Place your embroidery squarely and centrally over the mount board. Secure it by pushing the pins firmly into the edge of the board down the two shorter sides. Make sure the silk is stretched evenly.

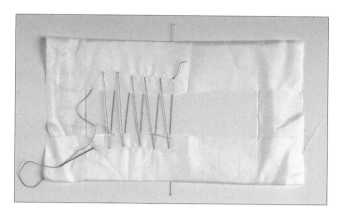

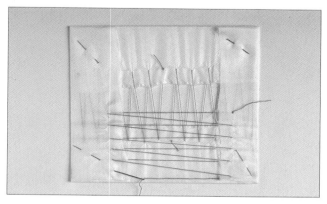

2. Turn the work over and start to lace the two longer edges together. Start in the centre and work towards the edge. Remove all the pins and pull the thread taut. Secure it with back stitch.

3. Fold the corners of the silk neatly and pin it in place. Repeat the lacing technique along the shorter sides. Check the front of your work periodically to ensure your embroidery is lying flat and square on the card.

Index

Bluebell Wood

*Strong, diagonal stripes of greens and blues
diminishing in size towards the distance give
depth to this embroidery.*